Astro's Adventures

Exploring Road Safety

By Tess Rowland

Astro's Adventures: Exploring Road Safety ©2024 by Tess Rowland
All rights reserved. It is not permissible to use or reproduce this material without the author's written consent.

In the event your book arrives damaged, please message me directly and I'll replace it for you.

tess@tessrowland.com

Book design, layout, and illustrations by Ken & Sherri Marteney.

Dedication

To my Uncle Joseph, whose wisdom and unwavering support inspired this book.

To my beloved dog, Astro, whose joyous spirit sparked this adventure.

And to those impacted by crashes, your resilience and strength inspire me to continue to fight for safer roads for all.

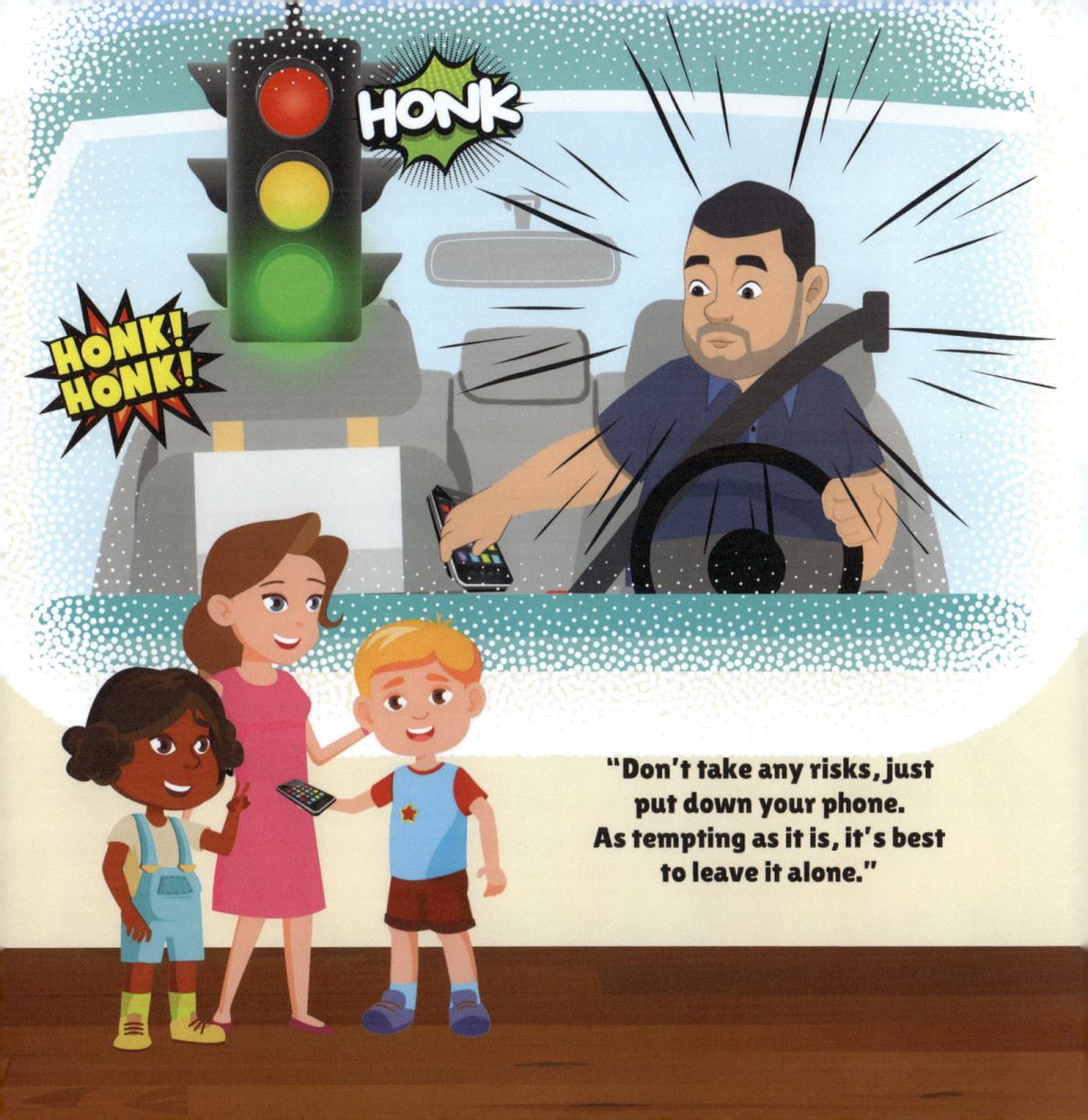

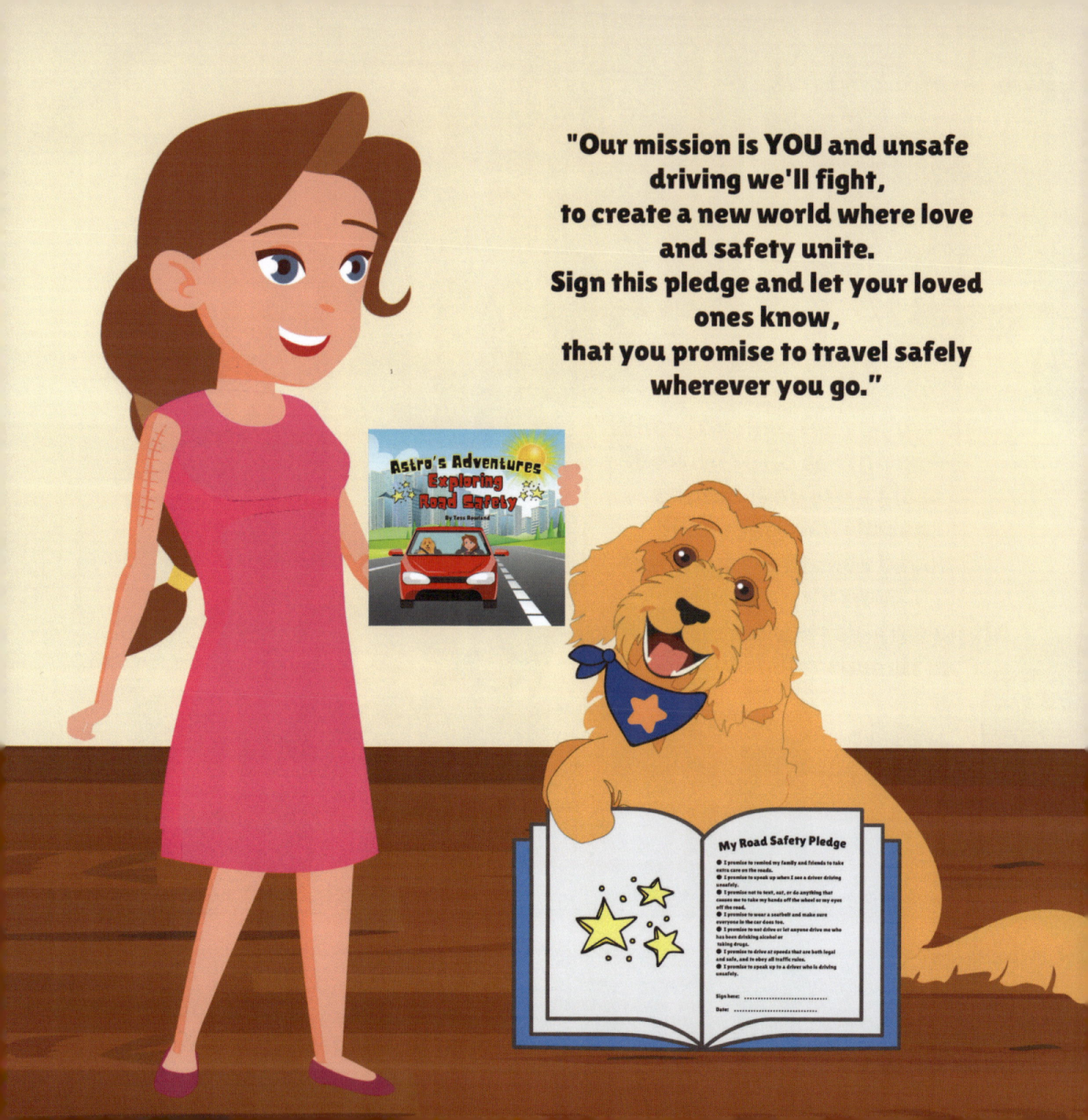

 **MY ROAD SAFETY PLEDGE**

> **I promise to remind my family and friends to take extra care on the roads.**

> **I promise to speak up when I see a driver driving unsafely.**

> **I promise not to text, eat, or do anything that causes me to take my hands off the wheel or my eyes off the road.**

> **I promise to wear a seatbelt and make sure everyone in the car does too.**

> **I promise to not drive or let anyone drive me who has been drinking alcohol or taking drugs.**

> **I promise to drive at speeds that are both legal and safe, and to obey all traffic rules.**

Sign here: ....

Date: ....

About Tess Rowland

Tess Rowland is an award-winning journalist and a passionate advocate for roadway safety. She served as the former National President of Mothers Against Drunk Driving (MADD), and traveled across the United States to educate communities about safe driving practices and advocate for legislation to enhance road safety.

For Tess, the mission for safer streets is deeply personal. Following a life-altering car crash in 2021, she made a profound choice to transform her pain into purpose. Harnessing the power of her own story, Tess has been a driving force in effecting positive change within her community. Her message to youth is one of resilience and empowerment: no matter the obstacles they encounter, courage and determination can lead them to triumph.

Tess lives in Houston with her dog, Astro. The two love exploring the city on long walks and spending time with friends and family.

Keep in Touch

tessrowland.com

Instagram, Facebook, and X @tessrowlandtv

Printed in Great Britain
by Amazon